MW01644240

Hers

Hers

Poets Speak (while we still can), vol. 2

Edited by Jules Nyquist

Beatlick Press
&
Jules' Poetry Playhouse Publications
Albuquerque, NM

Poets Speak (while we still can) is a series of mini-anthologies addressing the current national and planetary crisis.

Series Editor: John Roche
Associate Editor: Jules Nyquist
Art Editor: Denise Weaver Ross

Cover Design: Denise Weaver Ross

Special thanks to Beatlick Press publisher Pamela Hirst and Beatlick Press editor Deborah Woodside Coy

ISBN-13: 978-1545599013
ISBN-10: 1545599017

Acknowledgments

The following poems have appeared elsewhere:

Pamela Adams Hirst's "A new kind of lonesome" appeared on the *Watermelon Isotopes* blog, Jan 9, 2017.

Gayle Lauradunn's "In the Wrong Ghetto" was previously published in *World Order, 1969.*

Jules Nyquist's "Nasty Woman" appeared in *Duke City Fix Sunday Poem,* December 11, 2016 and is forthcoming in *Nasty Women Poets: An Unapologetic Anthology of Subversive Verse,* Lost Horse Press, fall 2017.

Kate Padilla's "Bitch" is a sestina that appeared in *Rolling Sixes Sestinas: An Anthology of Albuquerque poets.*
Jules Poetry Playhouse Publications, 2016.

Margaret Randall's "I Come from a Long Line of Women" is forthcoming in *The Morning After: Poetry and Prose in a Post-Truth World,* Wings Press, September 2017.

Denise Weaver Ross's "The Queen's Fire" appeared in *House of Cards: The Bone Suit,* a book of art and poetry by Denise Weaver Ross, 2017.

Denise Weaver Ross's "Spinning Jenny" originally appeared in *Midwest by Northeast by Southwest*, a book of art and poetry by Denise Weaver Ross, in 2012.

Georgia Santa Maria's "Apology to My Husband" is in her book *Dowsing*, Lummox Press, 2017.
Dowsing won the 3rd Lummox Poetry Prize.

Another World Is Possible!

¡Si, Se Puede!

The Equal Rights Amendment (E.R.A.), written in 1923, states:

"Equality of rights under the law shall not be denied or abridged by the United States or by any state on account of sex."

Preface

Hers is volume two of *Poets Speak (while we still can)*, a series of mini-anthologies in rapid response to the national and planetary crisis provoked by the election of 11/8/16. This series is the original idea of John Roche, series editor. Other 2017 volumes in the series are *Trumped, Water, Survival*, and *Walls*.

As editor of this volume, I have selected poems that address women's issues in various areas, divided into sections. Women's struggles are more important than ever since the Trump Administration took power in 2017. Section I takes us to the ice age, through Biblical stories, the Madonna, and on to how women are perceived in history, while still capturing that wildness inside. Section II explores women's bodies and self-worth with less than perfect bodies and the invisibility of older women in society. Section III continues those bodily images with what women endure with domestic violence and society, relationships, what we learn from our mothers or pass on to our daughters. Section IV brings us into the everyday life of women and girls, and how we find strengths at home, in the workplace or out in the world. Sections V and VI take on politics and world issues, especially since the Trump administration, the 2017 Women's March, the struggle to pass the ERA, reproductive rights and other issues.

Throughout, I find a sense of hope and solidarity that women will endure. We've been dealing with similar issues a long time and we're not about to stop now.

I wish to thank all the amazing poets and artists who are contributing to this project! The poems, photos and art in Hers truly come from the heart and I am proud to release this timely collection into the world as a powerful inspiration to all readers.

Jules Nyquist
Editor, Hers Anthology
May, 2017

Contents

III.

IV.

V.

VI.

I.

Spinning Jenny, by Denise Weaver Ross, Mixed Media

Lyn Lifshin

The Ice Maiden's 232nd S.O.S.

You wouldn't think that,
buried so long,
I could even respond again.
That I could hear sleet,
the branches over me
creaking and splintering.
Sometimes, I imagine
sun and light leaking through stone
that was a dream.
Then it was over.
I can't tell you how
I left what was my world for so long,
and that the first glimpse of sky
seemed like water,
my body like a pleated skirt
pressed under granite,
dark as violets,
rigid as bark,
terrified as I fell through ice crystals,
still as ice crystals,
seeing flesh and fingers
before I could feel them.

Katherine DiBella Seluja

Letter to Lilith from a Migrant Girl

I, too have wandered
Far from any shred of home.
Weeks at sea rolled the fear right out of me.
A wildness in their eyes, each little one
Wobbled off that boat. Their legs did not
Know land after so many green salt miles.
You too, knew lush and green. Sang the willow
Branches to the water. Taught the forest
To root and grow and hold. So many children
Lined the railing that first night. Bending
Deep over cold iron, letting loose
Any speck of home left inside.

Tani Arness

Daughter of Achan

> *Joshua Ch. 7: 19-25 The people heaped up a large pile of rocks over Achan's body. Then, in accordance with their principles, the people stoned the daughters also and burned the bodies to purge the land of evil.*
> *Verse 24: Then Joshua, together with all Israel, took Achan son of Zerah, the silver, the robe, the gold wedge, his sons and daughters, his cattle, donkeys and sheep, his tent and all he had. . . Then all Israel stoned him, and after they had stoned the rest, they burned them.*

Perhaps your father, like mine, could not resist the plunder,
the beautiful Babylonian robe, the silver coins and wedges of gold.
Perhaps he, too, was an unsatisfied man, pretending to be satisfied,
a man who hid things.
Did you see him bury it in the ground inside his tent
(the magic idol with golden tongue,
silver votives to decorate it, an expensive cloth to cover it)?
Maybe you, like me, watched him from the corner of your eye,
watching for your own way out?
Maybe all you knew were the prayers and meals he provided,
and you had no idea what constitutes a sin, a good man or a
bad one.

And when the people came to throw stones,
when your father lied about his innocence,
and your world exploded into loud rocks and accusations,
you had one moment to decide
whether to stand with him or run and hide—
Because, after all, it was his sin and not yours.
Or, is it true that the sins of fathers pass on, silently and without
arbitration,
to the pliable hearts of their daughters?

My father was a hunter. I carried his knives,
walked with him, hungry, through forests,
cut the necks of animals and skinned them for dinner.
And when he took just for the sake of taking, too much,

I was unable to stop him.
And when his buried idols called out to me,
I wondered how they knew my name.

And when the people came with stones and torches,
I stood frozen.
Perhaps you too have been called on to prove your innocence,
        only to find it missing.

Tina Carlson

Lillith

Let us begin the dismantling.

Ash stacks, scars that screech
In your dreams.

I upside-down on your.

Banish me o righteous ones.
Bear not the darkness in you.

Grease your souls with the exile
Of others. Fear me, wall me

Out, light me on fire.

I angel above the ravaging.
I hunker in your bunkers.

I crawl through your.

Shoot before you ask
Questions. Tower yourself

Before the fall.

I am you, feral. I am you,
Violent with vibrancy.

I owl the night of your
Silences. Rash your skin

With exuberance.

Patricia Roth Schwartz

Bear Girl

based on the legend that the Goddess Artemis
chooses girls to become her priestesses
who shape-shift into bears

When she was taken from amongst her sisters
to leave the snug chamber where they'd slept
so many nights in a pile, braided each other's
hair, whispered secrets guilty and joyful, dreamt
even sometimes the same dreams, she felt
betrayed, cast out, knowing it was her wildness
that had caused her exile, her failure to grow
into the kind of woman her mother valued, the one
who sat placidly chopping vegetables for soup,
who could remain for hours at the loom weaving
the patterns the market-browsers would pay for,
nothing too crazy or bold, her failure to become
the kind of girl who didn't run too fast,
play too hard, or let her voice, in passion
or anger, rise too high above the lulling tones
of her sisters--
                                        and so she found herself alone
at first, brought by night into a circle ringed
by torches whose tall flames threw shadows
over the faces of the oxen, the girls like herself
who had remained unbroken, not fit for kitchen
or hearth, nor the bed-chamber of the bridegroom,
girls who looked now in this light not even human:
as the drums began to throb like hearts, one turned
into a hawk, fearless, another, eyes deep as pools,
a deer, the one next to her, who reached out
with a touch as comforting as the favorite sister
she'd left behind, a kind of cat, soft yet
strong; even the bristly one who didn't seem
kind, quilled like a porcupine, beckoned her
at last to join the circle in which they began
to dance, in which they began to chant

in syllables alien yet familiar as the blood
through her veins, a language she remembers
from a time before her birth--
                                                            and it comes
to her now, as fiercely as the energy that wraps her,
strong as the arms of the mother she misses,
that she is here to *be* bold, to be crazy
and loud, to protect the sisters just dressing
now at home, taking out their ribbons
and scented oils—she is here to *be* wild:
the world they all love and live in and hold
in their hands, that grow now curved with sharp,
long nails touched with soft down, depends
upon it.

                    She--and the women who have become
her family now--circle together, and begin to growl.

for Eclipse

Lyn Lifshin

But Instead has Gone Into Woods

A girl goes into the woods
and for what reason
disappears behind branches
and is never heard from again.
We don't really know why,
she could have gone shopping
or had lunch with her mother
but instead has gone into
woods, alone, without the lover,
and not for leaves or flowers.
It was a clear bright day
very much like today.
It was today. Now you might
imagine I'm that girl,
it seems there are reasons. But
first consider: I don't live
very near those trees and my
head is already wild with branches

John Macker

*In Santiago's Hallway**

La Llorona searches nightly forever
for her two drowned children
her long black hair glistens like death's
waterfall under border lights.
Pale faced and riven with guilt,
she haunts the river
scans obits freshened with war
returns to the shrine of Santiago's hallway
where she's honored as
                                        monstrous
                                                  beautiful
                                                            post-modern
                                                                    black lit with *duende*
weeping mother
temptress, love sick killer
skeletal Madonna/
                                whore of the desert

as fixated on death as a skull.

Santiago holds the skull cane
he conjures her many meanings in his life
he can feel her eternal presence
he implores El Paso to return her
children from their watery graves

She still breaches the wind
with infamous bereaved wails.

* *Narrow hallway as mini-art gallery at The Rock House, café & gallery, El Paso, TX., featuring numerous artistic renderings or interpretations of the long-dead mother, mythical La Llorona, who haunts the borderlands to this day, grieving loudly for her children.*

Mary Dudley

Lupe

(to our little sister, la virgen de Guadalupe)

Were you sweeping the floor
in your mother's kitchen,
thinking impure thoughts about Jacobo
when that dodgy guy showed up--
the one who said he was an angel--
with the sketchy story about
god's baby already in your womb?

Didn't you have dreams of your own?
A home?
a garden? A small vineyard, perhaps,
with purple grapes, plump,
yielding wine sweet as a kiss,
babies of your own?

They gave you to an old man;
no one questioned his intentions.
You bore that boy—neither his nor yours—
raised him up to see him killed.
To that, you gave your life.
No one asked you if you would;
you did as you were told.

But now, Lupita, look!
People wear your image on gold around their neck;
in pins on their jacket,
They've made a goddess out of you--
a princess, a queen, is what you are;
why, they hang your picture
from the mirror in their car.

You're on potholders, little sister!
and on tote bags and pillow tops.
Prisoners wear you inked upon their chest
where, when they fight, fists batter you.

You bleed.
But everyone's your fan.

No, you didn't get to choose your life,
but, look, Lupe! you're a brand!

Mary Dudley

Half

When I was young, most prayers
were in the father's name and in the son's,
as if there'd been no mother
in that family of faith.

There *was* the holy mother
and my friends and I, we prayed to her.
We thought she'd understand
how people could be cruel,
how boys could take your love
and break your heart.

Like all the girls I knew, I lit candles too and
prayed novenas, said the rosary;
I wanted Mary on my side, to pitch my pleas.
I thought if she had made her boy
turn water into wine to keep a wedding happy,
maybe she would help with my exam, my dad,
my senior prom.

The prayers at church and home
were in the father's name and in the son's
as if there'd been few women in that family of faith,
no daughter, not a single sister,
just one mother,
just a single one.

And now?

Well, now I know that half the truth's no truth at all.
If you hear half a story, you'll never get it right
and what you think you know is wrong.
What's not there colors all that is.
A sum's not greater when you leave out half the parts.

To hear the truth about a story you need to make it whole.
You need the other voice,
you need the woman's soul.

Dwain Wilder

I Hear Momma

Y'all hear momma crying?
Singing? Down the bottom of that well?
The well she dug to get water
to birth you, suckle you?

She still down there, singing,
tears of all sorts,
clothing herself then ripping it all off.
All of it. Then
stitching the pieces together again
into raiment to keep herself and you warm
as she carries you naked
through the world.

You thought she had stopped doing that.
You thought she was dressed in such finery.
But that is not the rags she has rent
and mended daily all her life.

That glows from someplace else
all the sacrifices she made carrying/birthing/
carrying/birthing/carrying/birthing her loves—
no matter how neglected you felt
on that Tuesday forty years ago
when she had no patience
with you or anything else for that matter,
there she was, in all her majesty.

And she still down the bottom
of that well, once her own body,
down in the guts, near your navel
still singing, crying
still crazy with tearing and mending
somehow still carrying you birthing you.

Celeste Helene Schantz

New Madonna

Visiting a gallery of religious art

I can no longer relate to these dusty
framed virgins and whores. Your Madonnas
are too beautiful; poor, pale, mute dolls
propped against empty cerulean skies.

I want to see some new Madonnas. Of the scars,
of the streets. Our Lady of Goodwill, hunched
at the donated clothes bin. Show me
Madonnas of the long dark night. Our Lady

of Trafficked Saints, protector of school girls
stolen on the cruel road to Damascus.
Render me defenders of girls shot in the head
for being girls. Show me the Malala Madonnas.

Take the apple from Eve's hand. She never
asked for that prop in the first place, obvious
as a smoking gun thrust into a pedestrian's hand
as the robber runs away. Feel free

to put that snake away, too. Eve lives with you
amidst earth's clatter, sewage, bullets.
Eve is Sarajevo, Sudan, Syria, South Central L.A.
and Appalachia. I could show you

the bleak chiaroscuro of a sister trudging home
from her second job in night's dull neon; I'd
shade asymmetry and contrast in her unequal pay.
Color it in napalm, cinder, cement. I'd blend

warm color into her skin…give her some sturdy hips.
Ah, men, you should have shown them as real
women. For this hour, this unjust afternoon,
wags on. Eve and Mary, step down

from that cracked canvas. The distant sun
is lowering behind the trees. Go put on something
bright, happy and yellow. It is time, high time
for these weary sentences to be done.

Denise Weaver Ross

The Queen's Fire

The lives of queens
have ended with beheadings,
a poison asp at the breast,
and the fire of sati.

Not only queens,
but girls have burned
with the voice of God
in their mouths, women
drowned as witches for healing
the sick, and babies mutilated
to carve away the pleasure
from their own bodies.

Burning with every turn
of the wheel, we ignite
new wings and fly.

**Sati (or suttee) is an obsolete Hindu funeral custom, once practiced primarily among the higher castes, where a widow immolates herself (voluntarily or by force) on her husband's pyre.*

Tina Carlson

Something Wild

Tap tap tap on glass and the girl whose jeans and tee are already on, jumps out of bed, through open window onto the wet grass. A band of girls illicit in the night. Twelve years old, they trespass the provinces of boys: football fields, mud pits, frog ponds. Dark makes the air seem thick with sound. The quick breath of bats, a breeze. The girls become something wild together; dance the town away while it sleeps. At pond's edge they sing with the croaking frogs. Three girls fall into the muck. Dripping, they lie on the field and look up. The sky opens into its own vast and ephemeral light. Let them name the constellations they know: *Orion, Dippers, Cassiopeia* and the rest are their own invention: *Broken Tooth, Horse Hoof, Piano Bench.* As if the gossamer light of those stars could anchor them to the spinning top of their world.

Denise Weaver Ross

Spinning Jenny

There's a tornado on the high desert plains.
I ride it out, eye on the center.
The barbed wire fences around me
as I whoop and holler, swinging my partner
around and around and around.

They say it's all quiet in the center.
I don't know, but I reckon
I've heard a rumble or two.
Maybe I'm riding too close to the rim.
I circle out to my corner and to the center again.

Spinning out here on the high desert wind,
I feel the most at home.
I swing through space, arcing again and
again until I'm simply homespun –
a spinning jenny dancing the whirling dervish
with veils opening around me.

II.

Photo by Kevin Zepper

Judy Grahn

Comfort food

Piece of warm bread, buttered,
slathered in sticky amber:
miraculous menstruations
of bees.

Eggs, shells shattered,
scrambled, golden, fluffy,
plated: amazing menstruations
of ducks, chickens, geese.

Plucked, washed, crated,
assembled as red, orange, purple jams:
multiple yummy menstruations
of bushes and trees.

Erin Lynn Marsh

Disability Isn't Sexy

It is showing up at your boyfriend's office
wearing nothing but brightly colored
sneakers—the left one built up
one and a half inches to improve your gait—
and a trench coat. Your flowered cane
is propped against the wall because you need
both hands to unbutton the coat, reveal
your naked body: matching tangles of scars
at the hips, raised blooms to set off pale,
freckled skin.

***

It is being unable to grab your lover's
hand, walk side by side to your apartment door.
Holding hands—the physical connection
of his fingers covering yours—turns
violent. Limping tosses your body away
from his. Now the purpose of his grasp is to keep
you upright, on equal footing.

***

It is equipment. If it weren't for the blue
four wheeled walker—complete with black
plastic seat in case you tire—and your bouquet
of multicolored canes, you would have been able
to fit a king-sized bed. When he enters
the bedroom, the red scarf you've draped
over the lamp doesn't fool him. He tells you
it still looks like a hospital room. When you display
your naked body across the quilt, he tells you
it still feels like he's bedding someone's grandmother.

Erin Lynn Marsh

The Walker Keeping Her

upright, steady, is more than most men
can take on. That metal frame gleams,
always one step ahead—makes it impossible
for a man to sweep her off her feet.
She can't get caught in the moment.

A man needs her to be vulnerable,
needs to somehow disarm and keep
her off balance—knowing love
thrives only when one misstep
could mean crashing to the floor.

She knows her walker will keep her
safe. She also knows no man will choose
her balanced, upright life
when what he craves is a woman
who can fall and fall again—nicks
and bruises proof of her tussle with passion.

Lindsay Brenner

Three Poems

1.

the burden of female:

wear and act right

behave, appear

deny and battle the nature of age

makeup the self

pluck, shave, dye, constrict, constrain, trim, compress

compelled to feel inside and out as inadequate always

2.

modern single mother:

an urban huntress

daily daring the battles

fierce
outside her den

nurturing, soft
in the dwelling of her young

insuring the continuation of her offspring

dichotomy of two necessary femmes

she is woman

3.

red:

cycle of female

flowing, marking the end of the girl

shameful and hidden

burden of pain

but,

to be celebrated?

as ebb and flow of life giving fluid

gift of femininity

red fertility symbol

the primitive distinction of the goddess,

who can grow life of her own body

Patricia Roth Schwartz

Woman Taken Unawares

from the sculpture by Edgar Degas by the same name

"A SUDDEN blow: the great wings beating still…"
--William Butler Yeats, "Leda and the Swan

the quotidian that is hers
(yet never hers alone)
lies now sharply cleft
between what-was and now:

before in an instant trembled
then fell completely away
from a lifetime in which
she had trusted the rituals
of bodily joy: that every day
she would arrange her hair,
adoring its heft, wet
in her hands, twisting
as she pleased the fat braid,

that she would step
from her bath
worshipping as she should
the sheen of her own skin,
the turn of her calf,
the way her breasts fell
gently before her,
an offering--

all of this taken now,
unawares
cast into another place

where her hair lies
rudely shorn, limbs stiff

dancer's arms
pinioned,
wings that cannot lift

fluent hands now mute
rigid in their vigilance,
the joining of the thighs
where they hover no longer
a giving place

neck held in a gesture
she will now never release,
watchful, seeking always
behind her the awareness
she might have used
as a bludgeon

--and so she remembers it,
in the still silence, that time
between the before
and now,
remembers how once her teeth
had pierced
the crisp skin of the world
the sweet juice running free

Roslye Ultan

Berahot, the Spiritual Valley

"Up the hill and through rain by a road unknown…" Anne Carson

The truth is she's gone to where orchid fragrances
permeate the air, and thrive on
every green centimeter of space

A stranger came, unexpectedly, one Sunday afternoon, called her
from the glade along the southeast wall of her house
a sacred place rooted in 40 years of desire

Somewhere, someone travelled toward her obstructed breath
as she cleared moss asleep in the shadows
drops of red soiled her garden gloves

She passed away on the emergency-room table quietly, amiably --
Unobtrusively as she spent each day of life
cultivating each orchid species' needs for
light and water

The truth is she's gone to where the aroma of pecan tartlets
compete
for attention with turkey roasting in the oven
a drooling terrier on her lap till the
timer rang

Come away with me – drops of red soiling her apron –
You haven't time to call Elaine
Come, come away with me

The new baby won't have a hand-knit sweater on its first outing
No hand-embroidered table-cloth spring holiday
Apples will fall to the ground for rabbits
and squirrels

The truth is she's gone off with the mature charm of a cattleya
orchid
Able to adapt and grow anywhere, under any conditions
Drawing down spiritual energy

Yet, still remembered the twelve blooms
of phalaenopsis orchids, like moths in flight
perfumed the house for 40 days and nights

The truth is she's gone beyond terrestrial orchids…
to *Berahot, the valley* where orchids grow in air

Janet Ruth

Swift Angels

Mom was the unstated backbone of the family.

> *I meant to write about the bobolink,*
> *but the chimney swifts hijacked my thoughts.*

Unlike Dad, a Gilgamesh-type,
Mom never thought of herself as the heroine of her own story,
let alone anyone else's.

> *No elaborate plumage,*
> *just a sooty brown to match roosting sites that*
> *gave them their name.*

Yet as a young woman from a Nebraska farm in the 1950s,
she accepted a call to gift her secretarial skills to the church,
first half-way across the country in Pennsylvania,
then half-way across the world in Europe, where
Dorothy Gale met Gilgamesh.

> *They chirp and twitter madly overhead,*
> *little feathered cigars with wings.*

As a child, I heard her rise before winter dawn,
tiptoe downstairs to turn up the thermostat,
then the "ping-pong-ball-bouncing" sound as
heated water rose into the radiator in my room.

> *Twisting and turning through the heavens,*
> *aerial acrobats capture insects to feed chicks*
> *in nests plastered to the inside of chimneys.*

A mean word never passed her lips.
Mom lived a frugal life—recycled plastic bags,
sewed her own cloths. She taught me to sew,
no easy task since I did not inherit her patience.
After retiring she learned to quilt and gifted us all.

Avian scythes slice the sky above my head
into twisting ribbons of cerulean.

A slip of a woman under the best of circumstances,
the surgery and the cancer reduced her to a
featherweight of her former self.

From high in the sky
a coffee-colored feather
drifts on the wind,
floats into my trembling hand.

I sit at her bedside with my brothers and sister,
stand watch beside her. The well-loved life force contracts
within the barely recognizable shell of her body,
concentrates for one last brave act.

The evening is drawing close like a blanket.
I look up into the heavens—
filled with a host of circling, fluttering swifts.

Then the labored breathing ceases.
There is silence.
This tiny, unassuming woman—
iron bond with our past,
gentle arms that cradled us all,
who sent us into the world on our own adventures,
has escaped.
She marshalled the strength for one final leap
into what was for her, not unknown.

I don't know how to balance
celebration of her life
with the grieving.

The setting sun illuminates their brown-feathered heads,
transformed with golden halos.

Holly Wilson

Women of the Sacred Blood

In the temple they are holy,
Reserving themselves
Once a month
To replenish the Earth

Those most blessed
Bleed for the full moon,
Going naked into the fields
They leave drops of blood
By the roots of each plant,
The ground trembles
With a fastness
Rivaling infinity

They go in darkness
To keep the secret
And not offend the Father
Who prefers rising in the
morning
To find the work already done

Women alone
With their Mother and Sister
Keeping urns of blood
In the temple for curing,
When they dress in the
morning
They catch seeds
In the folds of their robes

Gayle Lauradunn

From Colorado to New York

The IUD had to be removed
before the bloody mass

That clump she had been
assured would not occur

The child at home awaits
her. The child she wanted
planned for   ached for

the blossom she inhales

She cannot feed another
clothe another
she is alone and must find a way

The machine sucks
out the mass

Cramps surge then cease

She has travelled 2,000 miles
to defy the law

and leaves the clinic
weightless   free

Lisa Alvarado

Limbic 2

These are nightmare words
lump
breast
breast lump
They are relentless.
The body in rebellion
is not soothed
by platitudes
or good intentions.

The light in the operating room
stares down, unblinking,
witnessing who passes through
and what will be lost.
I lie on the cold table
and watch the doctor enter.
Good girl.
Good soldier.
I am motionless
as he makes his cut
with the knife
as thin as a smile.

He cuts more than flesh.
The wound itself cries
Woman.

Eliza Mimski

At Seventy

I like my body
I mean, it's not the body of a young girl or even a middle-aged woman, but so what?
I'm old. My skin is old and it hangs, dramatically sagging
It folds into herringbone pleats
It falls into patterns that it never used to
It sighs

My chin, my neck, my stomach, my back the most
My chin is crumbling but I love it
My neck is corded but I love it
My stomach is dimple deluxe and I love it
My back is shifting and I adore it too

There is no going back with 70-year-old skin
My inner thighs – I think they call them crepey
Meaning wrinkled, elephant grandma skin, but I prefer not those words

Besides, elephant skin is grand
It is fascinating as a fingerprint
It is matron skin
And crepey?
That's just my skin deciding to be artistic,
Throwing a pucker party

I will keep my skin
I will keep my age
I will keep my body
I will celebrate it
Because my body is mine and therefore
It is beautiful

Pamela Adams Hirst

A New Kind of Lonesome

I feel like that astronaut that came back to earth recently, after a year in space. When asked what was the most surprising thing he learned he said, How long a year really is.

Counting in years now, how long my lover has been gone; counting in wrinkles now, the pain and disappointment transferred to my face,

As the French say, kindly, "a woman of a certain age" that I have become. Losing my youth, losing my home, losing my ace in the hole, I called him, has left me brittle, fragile, without moorings, the things that defined me within my own mind.

I'm Nernie's daughter, Debbie's sister, Beatlick Joe's girlfriend, I grew up in Vultee, Gloria was my best friend. But people die, the neighborhood changes and the landscape blurs. You have to start all over again.

It's a new kind of lonesome. And the memories have no substance to build on, what was was, and never will be again, any effort to recapture the past, is like chasing fog.

It was my choice to be live on the road, wake up in a different town every day. And with this, I became invisible. No anchors, no familiarities, everything is new, different, fleeting. I walk down the streets of Palm Springs, invisible; walk down Ocean Ave in Santa Monica, invisible; browse the Pasadena Public Library, invisible.

This is what aging is: losing everything, everyone. New generations replace touchstones and icons, yet one continues, seeking: what makes sense, asking: do I count, do I have value?

Anne MacNaughton

Widowed

when released from lifelong coupling
and focus shifts from some other
when one's naked consciousness goes about
the new world peddling itself everywhere
no cover no excuse

a shock to bruised sleep
dissipating some remnant each night slowly
exposing the surface of the soul
paring twinned aura
to single
responsibility
one would be wise

to misplace the soup spoon
sweep out the kitchen
let loose all the clattering cutlery
begin to set one's place
with a single, silent fork

III.

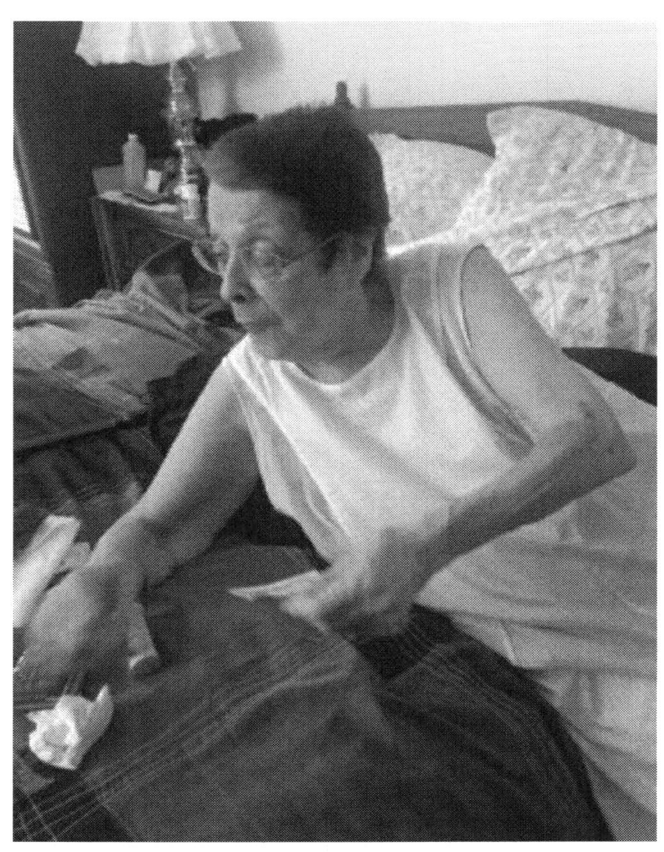

Angie
Photo by Lauren Schwartz

Margaret Randall

I Come from a Long Line of Women

I come from a long line of women
who silently counted to ten
or touched both sides of a doorframe
before entering or leaving a room.

I do not know if the men in my family
had these psychological tics
or what other small acts sustained them
through the years.

Acts such as taking what wasn't theirs
and making us promise not to tell,
building walls of secrets
around their privilege.

If they did have visible tics, they kept them
hidden: men neither confess
nor engage in odd behavior, at least
not where others can see.

Among the women, no one talked about
her own suspect quirks
although many told tales of others
as if they themselves were innocent.

Despite my best intention, I still dry every drop
of water glistening on faucet chrome,
do routine tasks in necessary order,
count before answering phone or door.

At eighty, I freely admit to these acts,
their power to keep me calm,
their harmless gifts of comfort
in a dangerous world.

Tina Carlson

Melanija

You knit
blue sweaters
in the green heart of
Slovenia.

Red cars shone,
silver, salami, snow,
armored eyelashes.

You tied your girlish notes
to pieces of yarn and floated
them above the concrete. Your
father the mouthy mechanic,

your mother made dresses
of flour. Snow covered what
was done and not said with
tire irons and trains.

Floor plans for
the masses, or
fortune. You knit and knit
until you were
blue. Perfume ads
in purple lockers.

You never let him touch
the children. When you say
he is a good man
your diamond
earrings flash their toothy
grins. Your spoons,
your alterations.

Speeches are
shoes, simple
to tie up with bling.
Hostage the
stolen words.

Colleen Powderly

Battering: The Women's Shelter

1
Reedily thin in white and gray
discreetly covered collar to shin
sitting primly in that noisy place

Jagged like diamonds
words small-voiced out

He sent her to ice covered streets
glistening sleet to turn a trick to feed
their need for white powdered dreams

His words were bold, pushed her out in the cold
Whose gon' want a skinny little bit like you
sell it on the street you dirty little nothin' whore?

One night a man whose voice blocked light
brought powder to deal for what she thought was her right
she heard her name cold as they rolled a joint,
held forth on the virtues high in her thighs
bags for safe whoredom more bags for no condom

2
Ankles crossed, fingers clenched
she picked her skin where she held the hate
I keep scratching myself, I know I'm lost
I can't tell where I end and where he starts

We spoke the words that led to freedom—
he called, she left them in the chair
We wrote them down so she could read them—
she lost them halfway there
We spoke again so she'd believe them—
she forgot some out of fear—

But she remembered enough to hear
excuses for hitting, then for twisting
her to a likeness she couldn't bear—

So we talked again and one night she went
and once more he screamed
Why you go back there?
You belong to me, not those lyin' dykes
tell me why do you go BACK?
She stood up, looked at him proud
Because I <u>want</u> to! she said out loud
Because ***I WANT TO!*** *And I'm going now!*

She grabbed the child, slammed the door
walked away despite his roar
I'm not a whore, she yelled. *Not anymore!*

And in the morning when I saw her
she knew she'd never see him again

Eddie Swayze

Rainbow Wings

For thousands of years, they hid in cocoons.
Couldn't spread their wings. Couldn't even fly.
Slept in the dark like cities without sun, dormant without dreams,
        ice-cold for years.
Snow hugged their cocoons.

They pushed their walls though difficult to do.
Some ripped them open but too few.
Some slipped into the light for a little bit but cruel society mocked
        them.
They slipped back into their cocoons.

Then one summer year, they had enough.
They ripped their cocoons into shreds.
Threw stones and bottles, and set the streets on fire.
Flapped their wings in rainbows and blew cruelty away.

Years came by, many cocoons thawed and opened.
Many of them spread their wings and ascended into the air.
They tasted freedom, delicious fruits and they savored them all,
        sweet with great boon.

Yet they looked back over their shoulders and remembered the
        others who couldn't come out.
They pondered upon sheer suffering, then turned their heads back
        in front of themselves,
And dreamed for the better.

They flapped their rainbow wings through the societies though
        hard work against great challenges.
They twisted the nuts and bolts to fix however nasty the tasks had
        to be.

They refused to surrender, for they wished upon the better for the
future generations.
They painted the rainbows on the future generations' wings.
They said, "Shall your wings flap stronger in brighter rainbows for
many years to come.

Megan Baldrige

Cuidado, Young Moms

If your boyfriend is 19,
if he is unemployed,
do not
let him babysit
the two-year-old,
who is not his daughter,
while you go to work,
even if he is charming,
and your daughter loves him.

Recently,
boyfriends
have blinded, beaten, burned, bitten,
dropped, kicked and raped
the babies.
Some died,
some survived damaged,
And you, young mother
will be blamed.

The babysitter reports
the baby was bad,
tore off a messy diaper,
refused to stop screaming,
would not take a nap
during football,
didn't go to bed on time,
dropped a shoe in the toilet,
ate the meth.

Babies do things
they later regret.
They rush into
precariousness,
teetering on balconies,
in seconds.

They are wily,
not wise,
they do not apologize.

Boyfriends,
Stop volunteering for baby duty!
Man up,
Find work.

Girlfriends, pay Grandma
to watch the baby,
to keep the baby safe,
to keep the boyfriend out of prison.

Police officers,
if the boys aren't working:
Bring out the safety net,
lock them up during the day,
when the moms ARE working.
Until the babies are old enough
to defend themselves.

Moms, try this:
a contract with the boyfriend.
Sex continues,
as long as the baby is unharmed.

Gayle Lauradunn

In the Wrong Ghetto

As I lock my front door
(wheretofore I didn't think of
it)
and walk down the side-
walk

            stares penetrate
not my back
but my

            face
my
            eyes
directly demanding to know
what
            I
am doing

                        here
and I can't answer.

Alone in my evening living-
room (thinking it no different
than previous
ones)
I am reminded of
my presence
                        here

by the solitary contralto
or bass
occasionally wandering by
            outside

free in its
unwhitened soul to be

beautiful and
self-sufficient
not asking me

                    why

I am here—
                    indifferent

that I am.

Liza Wolff-Francis

Once

years ago, I woke up
in the middle of the night
on a Greyhound bus
with a man's hand riding up my thigh.
The bus dark, I didn't want to wake anyone.
I picked up his hand, moved it from me,
but didn't know how to tell him to get away.
Years later I heard he was running for president.
And was elected.
But he is not my president.

Once, in a bar lit by fake candles and dim lights
a man grabbed my ass in an "I have you" way.
I slapped him and told him not to touch me.
He spent the night circling me, trying
to get my attention, to get me to be with him.
Then I heard he was running for president
And was elected.
But he is not my president.

Once, outside an ATM machine, after it was dark,
a man stood in the shadows,
watching me in the light.
When I came outside, he moved in front of me
so I would have to pass him.
He said, You want to fuck?
His voice like a snake.
Then I heard he was running for president
And was elected.
But he is not my president.

Once, I had a crush on a guy
we started kissing and fooling around
His hands up my shirt
His hands on me
Then he tried to stick it in me.

I told him I didn't want to
You know you do, he said.
Then I heard he was running for president
And was elected
But he is not my president.

I spoke up about these incidents,
said they were wrong.
I used the words sexual assault, harassment, rape
I said sexual violence
and the man to hold the highest office of our nation
called me a liar, said he would sue me
if I didn't shut up. And I was scared
again, because everyone believed him
instead of me.

Jane Lipman

A Woman and Her Window

A woman's life happened as she sat staring
out the window
into distances….

She knew where she was—*on her sofa*
dreamily drifting out of her life—

the children, like off-screen voices
asking questions, *What should I play, Mommy?*

I don't know.

She tried not to think beyond dinner.
Wanted to lose herself—

be a trellis of rose, tiered rock,
forsythia angling outward,
storm light quietly exciting.

At dinner her husband talked, or raged.
At breakfast and lunch there was her window.
The children laughed or cried or fought.

If she could pass from her body into cirrus,
into a soft evocative rumble of thunder,
or into some interior presence,

or the far-off places of a novel,
if she could be far, far away
             she could stay here.

Julie Dunleavy

George

She is sixteen
run from home,
the abuse, you know.
Now, she has to make her way.
A pimp sees her, recognizes
she is one of the girls.
All her sisters on the street
once ran too. Where were
they to go?

There is spunk in her.
Nothing can be worse,
she says,
than what she ran from.
"I'm in charge,
not a victim anymore,"
she says,
"I call the shots
on that bed in a rented room."

Up her sleeve, a switch
blade. Sure she'll use it
if trouble finds her
on a shadowed street
or in a parking lot.
Confident and ferocious,
she says,
"No one messes with
me anymore."

Inside her back pack
is her Teddy Bear.

IV.

Collage by Jules Nyquist

Joanne S. Bodin

Torn Nylons

The tape recorder plays the desert winds
like a vinyl record with deep grooves and scratches.

It plays words that slither down her thigh
like torn nylons from her past.

She tore apart her nylons the day
she said, "I do."

Torn nylons were her way of marking
the occasion while she sat in the passenger seat

of her boyfriend's Nissan Sentra—
the day the numbness would box her into

a predictable future
like moldy bread pudding or stale

family memories that sit on
Melmac plates too long.

She clenches her teeth, rewinds
the tape, listens to her lament one more time

then walks out of the motel room
where desert stillness washes away the last ten

years of her chalky past.
She plants bare feet in cool desert sand while

night breezes beckon her toward uncharted
territory and numbness scatters in winds

of change, and torn nylons take their rightful place
in the folklore of distasteful memories.

Herb Kauderer

Map of Lies

the sky is azure and the house smells of beans

they promised her a career
if she went through their education

an education that did not acknowledge
obstructions placed due to her gender and accent

without reference
to a daily context without wealth

the fireplug is opened for children to stay cool

now they court her vote
conservatives and liberals
and write news articles about
the apathy of voters

her father still landscapes for a living
"the smell of fresh-cut grass is as rich as I'll get"

news articles that might as well be sent
to a vacuum as to her people
who know the hard truths

sweat or crimes, poverty or incarceration
she cleans their houses, shops for their food
and dreams of poison

Herb Kauderer

Who Pays the Tallyman?

Orange Julius pouts
about overweight women

jokes about dating his daughter

brags about the wives of others
he has bedded

represents the political party
of 'family values'

acts to turn women into property
and expresses surprise
at our outrage

counts more people at inauguration
than at Women's march
because women don't count

neither does Orange Julius

Mary Elizabeth Lang

Amineh, the Track Star (a pantoum)

They say I'm going straight to hell
if I don't wear *hijab* to school—
Coach Laura says it's in the way,
it blocks my vision while I run.

If I don't wear *hijab* to school
the other girls won't laugh at me.
It blocks my vision while I run,
it slips and shows a bit of hair.

The other girls won't laugh at me,
"a race horse in a blinker hood."
It slips and shows a bit of hair—
could that inflame a man's desires?

"A race horse in a blinker hood"—
in running shorts and track team tee.
Could that inflame a man's desires,
no matter that my knees are bare?

In running shorts and track team tee,
I stuff the scarf inside my gym bag.
No matter that my knees are bare,
my hair is blowing in the breeze.

I stuff the scarf inside my gym bag
(Coach Laura says it's in the way).
My hair is blowing in the breeze—
they say I'm going straight to hell.

Scott Wiggerman

Malala Mesostics

based on Malala Yousafzai's 2009 BBC blog entries

January 3

terrible dreaM
        yesterdAy
   military heLicopters
                    And Taliban
off to schooL
                    Afraid

January 5

                uniforM
                      weAr
             normal cLothes
                   insteAd
                  schooL
          of militant Activity

January 14

bad Mood
  becAuse
schooL
      wAs not reopening
     girL's
educAtion

January 18

so Many
kidnApped
poLice nowhere
parents Are scared
toLd the Taliban
Announce curfew

January 19

More
one neAr my house
schooLs destroyed
Authorities
doing Little
todAy someone killed

Feburary 12

My brothers
my fAther
could not sLeep
swAt woke up
my reLigious
educAtion

February 11

fM channel
sAid
poLice
stAtion
would resembLe
tAnker exploding

February 17

rooM
I sAw brothers
one had a heLicopter
the other hAd
a pistoL
made of pAper

Elaine G. Schwartz

Paseo en El Paso, 1945

Pushing the dark blue baby carriage
Miriam strolls through the *Plaza Central.*

Olive toned hands firmly grasp
the warm metal handle.
Black hair gently caresses the red peonies
embroidered upon the collar
of her beige linen suit.
Engorged breasts strain the buttons
of the jacket.

The hot Texas spring
challenges this midwestern bride.
Her feet, in fashionable pre-war pumps,
begin to swell. She finds relief
on the Spanish tile bench
encircling the alligator pool.

Miriam adjusts the baby's lace bonnet.
Brown eyes focused on her daughter's blue ones,
she doesn't notice the approach of the woman.

What a happy baby! So clean and fresh!
You take her for a stroll every afternoon?
You are a fine nanny.
I have two little ones at home.
I could use your services.
I'll pay you well.

Miriam smiles,
raises her head, momentarily
shifts her gaze to the woman.
Thank you.
I'm happy with my current employer.

Leah Zazulyer

At the Alive Center/Geneseo, New York

I
She can't come in
Don't you know
she has no bones
when she fell down
the stairs
she just crumpled
because she has no
bones
well the doctor said
no
she bruised this
one bone.

II
Case workers slip her
their own money,
try to tell her
about food stamps,
but she can't listen
because the phone inside
her stomach
keeps ringing
and she has to talk
to somebody.

III
Well she'll just live
in her car
its cozy
and plenty big
for one person…
but winter, they say,
and she stares
until the icy surface
of her eyes

cracks open
and deep water
runs swiftly.

IV
She needs help
she writes.
Every letter says
won't somebody help her.
P.S., she may go
dancing tonight.

Stella Reed

Red Shoes Redux

Men of religion wet
mouths agape   pig eyes
fat palms,

I'll dance on their laps
            for their sins
my second mouth so close

the bitter
fern breath of it catches
            in their gray nostrils.

Him leaning on his sword
            at the back
wants me   to believe

he's big as this pole I twist
on   something steely
            to hold   in two hands.

Oh sweet nothing of my soles
            faith is hard
            as floorboards.

See how their deep dipping
            fingers emerge red
                        staining the doors of the church

                                    I'm barred from.

Lisa Alvarado

New World Order

They call us criminals
as they stand in front of clinics.
They call us criminals
and sit in judgement on Capitol Hill.
They call us criminals
because we do what is forbidden.
We say women are not receptacles.
We say women are not breeders.
In their world,
they would pass sentence on us.
In their world,
we will kneel with coat hangers,
darkness covering us;
the dark flow of life
running down open legs.
In their world,
we will climb the narrow stairs
meeting shadowy men.
Men with scalpels
that sing with fear and old blood;
who will take our money
and promise to keep silent.
In their world,
I have done what is forbidden.
I am a criminal.
My crime is that I chose myself instead of a child.
My sin is that I am not sorry.
My sentence is I know I am not safe.

Jude Moore

Violet

today I read that it's less difficult to legally own a gun
in Massachusetts than it is to have access to Adderall
& also that a number of veterans who have lost limbs

run out of insurance after so much & turn to heroin
for the pain. for the lack, maybe, & today a Black boy
was shot by police for maybe holding a bb gun,

& a little girl I am teaching about glaciers, & evergreens,
& crowns asked if I had ever been in love. today
i told her yes but i couldn't explain you, or all

of what you were to me. two days ago my ex
sent me pictures of flowers from Amsterdam & it ripped
my guts to shreds, like someone's back after mortar

or how easy it is for bullets to rip through skin
or how simple it was for you to feel old enough to want
to die. they reminded me of you, & I am home—

in my old bedroom, where I grew up, sitting next
to your unopened box of letters. we were young
& on one you wrote *you're beautiful* 134 times.

today someone wrote a story about two girls
getting to be together forever, going to paris
& eating chocolate & reading camus & that wasn't you,

because you're dead, & it wasn't me, because you're dead.
today I read about vampires who are good & wasn't it you
who first told me that? *monsters*, you said, *were like angels—*

they used the same latin in the bible. in their holies. today
i taught a little girl latin & maybe one day she'll understand—
we made crowns for ourselves & sang about friendly dragons

& she doesn't know about mass shootings, or systematic violence,
or overdoses, or falling in love. we played with her dog
& we made lunch & in another world maybe in a few years

we would have had that all our own—a house & a dog & a little
girl
who hates wearing shoes & who loves summer. & maybe we
would have named her after stars, or gods, or flowers

Georgia Santa Maria

Apology to My Husband

Instead of cleaning house
for your cousins' visit tomorrow,
today I wrote a poem.
I really loved the poem.
Loved writing it, and loved reading it.
Loading the dishwasher,
not so much, I admit.
The bathroom floor is full of dog-hair,
and the toilet has a pink ring around the bowl
like a Texaco station, neglected on Route 66.
And the chicken juice from the groceries last week
is still puddled up on the refrigerator's second shelf.
Your bed, which they're supposed to sleep in,
has the same sheets it had six months ago
and no blankets.
You share your bedroom with the dog.
I won't be cooking tomorrow, either. You'll
probably have to get something to take-out.
I haven't shopped since the leaky chicken—
y'all might need some eggs or bread or milk.
I'll see you later—I'm taking my poem
up to Santa Fe and reading it to my friends.
Tell your cousins I said "Hello, and Best Wishes,"
and that I wrote you a poem.

Kate Padilla

Bitch

They say I'm a beast
And feast on it. When all along
I thought that's what a woman was.
They say I'm a bitch.
Or witch. I've claimed
the same and never winced.
— From "Loose Woman," Sandra Cisneros

Let me holler like a beast
screech and pull along-
side those *machos* who say I was
nothing but a bitch
but I fisted up and claimed
my place in line. I didn't wince.

Años pasados, I witnessed a woman wince,
forced to kneel before the beast,
whose tradition sanctioned his claim
on her as if she were property along
with his horses and bitch
dogs, but *we aren't what we was*

back then, when my mother was
told when to breathe, when she winced
afraid, when he called her bitch
a word he learned from other beasts,
macho men who went along
denying their wives' claim

for space where peace is claimed,
a safe place. She was
a trusting woman until he came along.
At first it was love, then she winced
after marriage when the jealous beast
struck her for being rich

in beauty and intelligence. From them a bitch
was born, a daughter who disputed claims
and customs, who stood against the beast,
embraced her mother who was
until her death afraid. She winced
at his presence, unable to challenge the long-

forged family norms of long-
ago. She was *nada*, never a bitch
who could make the tribe wince.
Her well-armored daughter claimed
her own voice, in her determination she was
fearless, prepared to take down the beast.

The daughter didn't wince. She stretched a long
rope and baited the beast, yelled, "I am a bitch."
Claimed the podium. She was not her mother, afraid.

V.

Photo by Gretchen Schultz

Sylvia Ramos Cruz

H.E.R.S.

Health. Economic Security. Representation. Safety.
Women's rights priorities- Women's March Global
Huffington Post, January 13, 2017

It's hard to know what goes on around the world,
in Burundi, Antarctica, Lithuania, Japan, but
I think the same game plays in all these places—
anywhere we see feminine faces.

A game of 3-Card-Monte, a constant shuffle to hide
the issues of our day— doors to plum jobs and boardroom
bathrooms barred, groping hands, leering lips, voices stifled,
lives lived lean in old age, after a lifetime of wages stolen.

Cards that hide the issues of our day— faced and numbered,
shaped and colored— cut to divert our eyes, turned to uncover
a new neighbor's plight, so we rush to lend a helping hand,
make the best of it for us, once more.

It puts me in mind of Kay Ryan's poem, *The Best of It*,
begs me ask, "Will there be a point as our acre is pared,
our garden whittled down to a bean, when we'll look
at what's left, realize, one more slash and we'll die."

***

In designer heels
and tennis shoes
in Lima, Reykjavik, Banjul
women's steps
cracking pavements
everywhere we see
feminine faces.

Cracking pavements
to get
their full acre

restored
for they grow thin
on a bean, no matter
how full of good
works they be.

Cracking pavements
to access
health,
economic security,
representation,
safety—
rights
with no gender,
rights
they already own
as full-blooded
members of the whole
human race.

To all of you,
Sisters, I say,
Don't make do!
Stop marching!
Rise up!
Grab what's yours!
Yell,
"These are OUR rights,
as much part of us
as our skin!
Would you have us
peel that off,
too?"

John Roche

Sevenling (after Akhmatova)

She died for three things alone:
Prairie wind from a horse's back, scent of sage in ceremony,
Water sweet on the lips.

She hated the idiot-faced greeter at Walmart
And hunger in her child's belly
And her own weakness.

She died from the water cannon's icy burn.

Susan Paquet

Red Skies at Morning Sailors Take Warning

Suffrage, Seneca Falls, and Lucretia*
Nantucket, ship captain's daughter
understood warnings from the sky
red at morning, omen of stormy seas
didn't give her a moment's pause, she marched on

My alarm calls me at 6:00 a.m. a century later
I shower, dress, pour myself a bowl of Cheerios
switch on the television and see it –
Donald's red tie on the morning news
my genetic inheritance from seafaring
Nantucket ancestors gives my neck a shiver
warning of dangerous waters ahead
I pray to God, we all don't drown

*Lucretia Coffin Mott – (1793-1880) abolitionist, suffragist

Susan Paquet

A Modified Sestina of a Modified Dream

Conceived below cracks of a tenement ceiling
mother's fourth child, not expected
Celestina bored with crayons, ran with scissors
in a house of broken dreams and glass
cigarette smoke's raspy whispers-
careful a girl could get cut

Fought like a boy, fists and upper cuts
fought on gritty floor below ceiling
fought like a girl words and whispers
Celestina's dreams were unexpected
rejected prince with slipper of glass
needed better shoes to run with scissors

Law school sharpened her mind like scissors
climbed success ladder, despite the warning whispers
made law firm partner, before expected
she had made the cut
heard sweet sound of cracking glass
as she crashed through that ceiling

Thirty years later she sits behind a mahogany desk, wearing a silk blouse. The long sleeves hide the scars, those made by the sharp glass of the ceiling she crashed. Running with scissors, still brings harsh whispers. A dream can be much more complicated than expected.

Merimee Moffitt

Women finally spoke up in the Seventies

Quiet in the Sixties, still didn't tell; we boomers compliant;
lots of good girls taught serve and smile
Girls these days drop the kiss-up face, whoa baby!
the grinning Mona Lisa and all her being nice. Back then: Oh, my
body?
Yes, sir. I'll be right with you; my brain, my life? I'm yours, I
guess.
Did our mothers know? Did they know raising a generation
of *revolutionistas*, *las feministas locas*?
a Hail Mary off the dead end of servitude, a catapult
out of solitude from a home not ours, but his;
we need attitude to achieve that stance. Thank you, Mom.

We unbound our breasts, let down our hair,
swirled in dance with the Earth bare feet—
we learned to give to ourselves, talk back 'n take no prisoners
—well, almost. We almost won, anyway.
My father rarely held a child, cooked a meal, swept the floor,
ironed shirts.
He mistook his penis for a power tool, a pliable key to ownership
admission to top colleges and jobs. It was a man's world and
we of the fifties, sixties, seventies, we were girls
then "ladies," then bra-burning-bitches, women.
Our daughters want
choice and pleasure in love and work;
women now yell, tell, and press charges. Our voice,
we want power pricks to put away their killing tools;
to love our mother Earth, no duh. Civilized, my ass! Our kids need
food and jobs not replacement parts—we women of the seventies
are done with naked emperors, bargain-basement atrocities
America, you are a woman, don't take it lying down—
don't let them scare you into silence, again. Don't be polite, again.

Ceinwen E. Cariad Haydon

More in Common

Equal is not the same as identical
but difference regarded equally

A Syrian mother said,
'I look to the future
but the future does not look back at me'

All things are contingent –
my hormones my race the colour of my face
my creed my saints my political complaints
the signs of my status my coping apparatus
my faults and my flaws my wounds and hidden scars
all things are chance I could be you you could be me
do you hear me do you see – me

See past my honeyed skin
the dress that I am in – the babe in my arms
cries like yours when in pain to fight is insane
share with me and I'll share too
in illness and in health we will work to pull through

Shut eyes deaf ears hard hearts pave the road to hell
if you help me and I help you we will do very well
equal in the sight of god the message is quite plain
the wisdom of the ages teaches share and share again

Jesse Ehrenberg

Remember the Ladies

The last thing Abigail Adams
said to her husband John,
before he rode off to the
Constitutional Convention,
was
"Remember the ladies".
His response was a quick, dismissive,
"Yes dear".

He was a man with
more important things on his mind.

And in Philadelphia,
when the delegates were discussing ratification,
someone mentioned "women's rights",
and, after a brief discussion,
they decided that it was already implied
in the phrase
"All men are created equal",
and besides,

they were men with
more important things on their minds.

And today
women are still ignored,
treated like children
unable to make their own decisions.
It's like there's
a war against women.
Just look anywhere in the world,
and you'll see
women desperate for a better life
sold into sexual slavery;
young girls kidnapped
and used as child brides.

And there's still
genital mutilation,
and women murdered
just for trying to get an education.

And it's centuries of
social indoctrination
that have led to a majority
being treated as a minority.
In the Media.
In the classroom.
In the home.
It's women's issues that
are always the unseen issue.
It's the war against women
that's always ignored.
And it's a war that
only 'the ladies' can end.
Because,
as we know,
men have
more important things on their minds.

Stuart A. Paterson

Today I Won't be Writing about Fairies

& how they live among an island's
small lovely flowers, or being Scottish,
or how I'm counting down the hours
until the sun appears, or my garden,
or the cat who purrs when I stroke his ears.

Today I won't be writing about being
a man or interesting anecdotes
about my travels in Myanmar,
its colourful locality, how beautiful
the children are, that time in Laos I saw
amazing sails, the way those sounds
& colours haunt me beautifully even now.

Today I won't be writing about Samia
Shahid. There is no need to talk of honour
& a killing in the same outraged liberal breath.
Such things speak for themselves in any
language, better than the likes of me can
when I can't even write of being a man.

Samia, originally from England, died while visiting relatives in her ancestral village of Dhok Khinger in Pakistan. Her family initially claimed she had a heart attack, but an autopsy revealed she had been strangled and raped. Her husband Syed Mukhtar Kazam repeatedly said she had been murdered because her family were angry that she had left her first husband, her Pakistani cousin Muhammad Shakeel, to marry him in 2014. Shakeel is currently on trial for her murder.

Kenneth P. Gurney

This Drawing of a Crow

This drawing of a crow you gave me
depicts the crow pecking out the word "men"
from the Declaration of Independence,
and possibly the constitution and the Bill of Rights
farther down in the sheaf.

This drawing made of thickened berry juice
applied on to the pressed remnants of crushed plant fibers
could have just as easily had the crow's beak
act as a stylist marking a preceding "wo" in elongated lines.

This drawing implies to me we are only equal in death,
for which the crow acts as metaphor,
and declared equality under the law
is just a fiction as is this picture is an artist's fancy.

This drawing does not address cultural biases
or millennial long traditions
or tribalism between races and folksy taxonomies
or the implications of holy books
whether cross-embossed or not.

This drawing could incorporate a woman
with a ball and chain upon her legs
adjacent to the crow with a broom and dust pan
standing on the elegant script of the founding documents
sweeping up eraser rubbings and ink blots
and the quashed political inspiration
of the Iroquois Confederation
with its matrilineal kinships and stewardship of the land.

I love this drawing—more for the idea the crow
plucks out the word "men" and leaves a blank,
like a fill-in-the-blank and each individual,
no matter their gender or racial mix,
receives a copy upon coming of age

and gets to write their own name into history,
into equality, into ten original guaranteed freedoms
that are now twenty-seven in number.

Martha Deed

I ask you is there anything new under the sun?

1

noun: **equal**; plural noun: **equals**

a person or thing considered to be the same as another in status or quality.
"we all treat each other as equals"

as in the Declaration of Independence?

that all men are created equal,

that one?

the lines of suited white males trailing across the antique
carpets in the halls of power today?
that we see on TV? those equals?

the lines of slaves weeding strawberries in Jefferson's fields
when those lines were written?
those things? (do you have to have male white skin
not to be a thing in 1776?)

> *If there be an object truly ridiculous in nature,*
> *it is an American patriot, signing resolutions*
> *of independency with the one hand, and with the other*
> *brandishing a whip over his affrighted slaves.*– Thomas Day[1]

are those the people we mean? Are those "affrighted slaves"
created equal?

should we admire Thomas Day for his vision?
or–

is he a sharp-eyed man on the one hand – and blind on the other?

. . . he
ventured to propose marriage on his old terms.
He required her to renounce all the vanities and
fashions of town life, even its moderate pleasures,
and to retire with him into some leafy seclusion –
where books and a career of utility and active bene-
volence should constitute her chief pleasures.
. . .
He allowed her to keep no female servant,
but required her to perform the various duties
of the household with her own hands, which she
cheerfully did. . . . she was passionately fond of music
and played sweetly on the harpsichord ; but this soothing
instrument and her music books were banished
at his strange request; not that he disliked the voice
of music or could not appreciate the harmony
of sweet sounds, but, in his opinion, they were luxuries
which might be dispensed with without serious loss.
"Besides" he would say, "we have no right to luxuries while the
poor want bread." This was almost too severe,
but she bore all with the most exemplary patience.
– John Blackman[2]

2

how much real estate must a white man own
before he is equal enough to vote?

Such is the frailty of the human heart, that very few men,
who have no property, have any judgment of their own.
They talk and vote as they are directed by some man of property,
who has attached their minds to his interest… – John Adams[3]

can Gutenburg and Google solve the riddle of mistaken equality
fueled by ignorance
spilling ancient arguments upon our brains that we may discover
the racket?

are we gullible or what? or are we merely uninformed?
do we not understand that the language of politicians
is aspirational at best?
that parsing is a political game?
that we the *bourgeoisie* are assets to be gulled?
hypocrisy our national religion?

will the winds still blow across the open prairie?
will the avalanche of proud ambition with no wisdom
bury us all in history's cemetery of bad ideas
before this poem is done?

Notes

1 Thomas Day. Fragment of an Original Letter on the Slavery of the Negroes, Written in the Year 1776. broadside. 1784. http://cdn.loc.gov/service/rbc/rbpe/rbpe14/rbpe146/14603200/14603200.pdf

2 John Blackman. Memoir of the Life and Writings of Thomas Day. 1862. pp. 80-81, 90-91.

3 John Adams to James Sullivan. On Women, the Poor, and Voting Rights. May 26, 1776.

John Roche

78 Grandmothers

When Sinjar was liberated
in November 2015
the Peshmerga uncovered mass graves,
one containing 78 Yazidi grandmothers.

When the black-clad conquerors arrived in August 2014
they sorted the Yazidi women by age, a simple triage:
The maidens to be sex slaves, their mothers to be servants,
their grandmothers to be shot or buried alive.

This poet will refrain from comparisons to the Rape of Nanking,
My Lai, Sabra and Shatila, or countless historical parallels. Neither
posit the Rape of the Sabine Women as the starting point of
Roman Civilization. Nor equate warrior culture, religious
fundamentalism, and patriarchy. Nor analyze the rise of this
particularly savage apocalyptic cult.

Only say, there is a grave in Sinjar
containing 78 grandmothers.

Only say, the poet's curse be on those who disrespect
grandmothers.

Only say, the poet's curse fierce and ineradicable be upon the heads
of those who slay the 78 grandmothers, and upon those who slay
the 778 grandmothers, and upon those who slay the 7,778
grandmothers.

May they be immediately rendered impotent and suffer a thousand
humiliations and torments, and may a coward's death soon follow.

Only say, may peace come to Sinjar, and children play with
grandmothers, and brides be dressed by grandmothers, and babes
be held in the arms of grandmothers.

Anne MacNaughton

GOOD GOD GERTIE
—YOU'RE COOL!

There
in your black robes,
grand mother
and father both
seated in the place reserved
for judgment. Smile
stretched flat
beneath the brow lined from
so
much
serious

Teach me, old lady,
the source
of syllable.

We could dream a pure tongue
of such antiquity
that each word would hold
its own history, tell
the time and place of its first breathing
release into human voice.

Let's start a dialogue
with creation—

Would we so honor
words
that we'd remember
how to enter the sacred
(thus)
with each speaking?

WORD
WORT ORTH W-
EYE-RD
EYE-ryne WARD-us
WERB-um—
TELL TELL-in
TOLD-ë ZELL-en
TOONG TONG-UE DIN-
gwah
—TUNG —WAH!

/ INITIAL LANGUAGE /

Living Syntax wherein
each time a word is said
the speaker adds to common
thread phonemic notes—

Gene a logy
of every mouth that's spoken it.

Shall we word it now
from the beginning, Granny?

The poet here, full of words

And you in your seat
black robes
white dog
your brow lined
with so much
cellular
s-s-s-syllable

VI.

Community Health Program, Bronx NY
Photo by Lauren Schwartz

Nickole Brown

Inauguration Day, 2017

Like that horse, how sick he was
but not so sick he could not walk.

And because he was big—nearly seventeen
hands—alive or dead he could not be carried,

so my friend who loved him best
had a hole torn from her pasture deep enough

to expose the reddest dirt, the kind that refuses
new water but holds still what seeps from below.

Then with great reins she eased him
into that grave. To understand, know this:

how his eyes went before his legs, how quickly
she had to scurry out once his gaze

lost focus and glazed, quickly before his knees gave
and all that proud weight slumped and crushed her

into the dark. Know that. And know this:
this is not a metaphor for another January day

but a swallow of the same obscene
grief, a sickening hush.

You see, the horse trusted her.
No one but her could have coaxed him

into that pit with its sticky, rust-colored clay.
Know how she was forced to stay calm

so the horse would not die
afraid.

Deb Coy

Poetic Justice

Josephine the poet
grabs Trump in the crotch,
twists the little thing.
She makes kissey kissey noises
then she looks him up
and down and side to side.
She scowls
loosens her grip, drops it,
"Two," she says, "maybe three
on a good day."

Eliza Mimski

The March for Reproductive Rights

Last night, on January 21, 2017, in San Francisco, in the pouring rain, while wearing a poncho, my shoes soaking wet and my fingers numb from the cold, I joined 100,000 others who are fed up with the pussy grabbing president.

I saw signs.
Dicks should not make laws about vaginas
Feminist as fuck
The resistance will be nasty
Women are powerful and dangerous
This pussy bites back
Girl power
My country went to the voting booth and all I got was this lousy misogynistic, authoritarian president
We will not go quietly into the night! We will not vanish without a fight!
Power of the pussy

I saw women
All ages and colors I saw all genders And men by the hordes

For a while I was frightened in the midst of the crushing crowd
It took me half an hour to make my way to the library to find my friend
We rode the elevator to the sixth floor and took pictures out the windows
All those people below, all those colorful umbrellas
We looked at each other
Can you believe this sight? Can you believe this night?
We sat in the hallway and ate our dinner
And then joined the crowd at the end where it felt less claustrophobic

Since the election I had been depressed and felt hopeless
This morning I felt the old me coming back
I was inspired
I felt supported
I felt close to women in a way I never had before

Kathamann

Marginalization

Marching
Again
Resisting the
Great forces
In the dark days of
National upheaval
Again
Losing ground as we step forward
I am fearful
Zillions of us bewildered
Again
Tired days from the past come back
In privileged bravado
Only white males need benefit
No more rights for the rest of us.

Karla Linn Merrifield

Cherita Triptych: Good Trumps Evil

In the new world order

we are readily expendable,
we old broads with walker or cane;

we post-fertility crones, we wrinkled lesbians,
we blacks, we browns, we reds, we yellows,
we whites— we destined for the landfills. But—

~~~

Primal dreads go unacknowledged,

so you abandon your humanity out of fear;
I have developed P.T.S.D. from the venom.

Violent poetry gathers force; poets are the first
to be hauled out and shot—Lorca, Mandelstam—
because our pens become nuclear weapons.

~~~

Nasty women write

tanka haiku renga cherita
all night every night

so nasty women can unite
to tell the story of Medusa's mirror
in freeing millions   among them the poets

Mary Dezember

Female Solidarity

(The seemingly impossible can be accomplished;
see the documentary *Pray the Devil Back to Hell*
about the women of Liberia stopping war.)

A woman may try and try and try
To break through
The wall of male dictates --
The illogical hegemony
That is reactionary rather than responsive.

She may try to break the wall
With kindness
Or with intelligence and knowledge
Or with skill and ability
And brightness and brains,

Or with harsh words,
With measured words,
With lullaby words,
With love.

She may walk the moated wall --
Sometimes filled with water,
Sometimes with eggshells --
Around and around and around,
Hoping it will fall like Jericho --
Tip toe, tip toe,
Do not wake the beast
And never be honest
Or he might feel his own self-provoked shame
And *on you* put the blame:

Heaps and heaps of blame.
Nuclear diplomacy blame.

A woman alone
Might try and try and try
To be seen as a *person first*,
Otherwise known as the
Birthright of men.

But no matter what, she is seen and treated
Not as a person,
But how a man defines a woman.

Personhood for a woman?
The 8 Ball says, "Outlook unclear."

But when women join together
In trust
To create and nurture
The poetry called *Life,*
With Respect
For every being --
Plant, animal, each *person*,
Our planet Earth --
Women become Jedi Extraordinaire Masters,

And *try* becomes *do, doing, done.*

H. Marie Aragón

Shoulders of Herstory: A Woman's Voice

"Men, their rights, and nothing more;
women their rights, and nothing less,"
Susan B. Anthony takes a stand.

She barnstorms for women's right to vote.
Her effigy dragged through the streets.

"Women will always be dependent
until she holds a purse of her own,"
Elizabeth Cady Stanton shouts.

Women in white marched.
Men threw tomatoes.
"Go home to your husbands,
babies   washboards   and irons."

"Look at me!"
"Ain't I a woman?"
Sojourner Truth asks
as she puts her foot in the door at Seneca Falls.

"I'm no lady,"
Jeannette Rankin, first female Representative.
"I'm no lady; I'm a member of Congress."
She was a force in passage
of the Nineteenth Amendment.

Hillary Clinton stands to say,
"Human rights are women's rights
and women's rights are human rights,
once and for all."
After the election women posted
I Voted stickers on Susan B. Anthony's gravestone.

Hillary concedes.
Trump toasts Putin.
Women march on Washington,
Nairobi, Paris, Mexico, London…

Merimee Moffitt

Politics and Pussy

In spite of facts like he can't read
He's Pro-life and shuns democracy
Don't take your guns to town, girls
Just leave your guns at home
In spite of every man a loaded gun
They'll chase you if you run, girls
In spite of he can't Roe v. Wade
Or EPA or ACA
Just run your reading thumbs to eyes
And push the blood around his face
Your water, air, and life's at stake
Remove your high-heeled shoes, girls
And use your feet to stand
In spite of how you know
IT's now, now or never ever
No, grab your words, and fight
In spite of vinegar eyes.
Do your duty, take a stand

Jules Nyquist

Nasty Woman Pantoum

I suppose I could have stayed home, baked cookies, hosted teas
but I've been labeled a nasty woman
If I was elected, I could have slept with an ex-President
the First Dude would have played sax full time

I am a nasty woman
Janet Reno's mother wrestled alligators
The First Dude would have played sax full time
Georgia said if I painted that mountain long enough I would own it

Janet Reno's mother wrestled alligators
My life broke in two right there, Mabel
Georgia said if I painted that mountain long enough I would own it
I am proud to wear pantsuits

My life broke in two, Mabel
I am fearless of the far side of fifty, Erica
I am proud to wear pantsuits with zippers
flying first class without fear, I'll escape to an island, I've had enough

I am fearless, long past the far side of fifty
Joan didn't sleep with any man who had a draft card
flying first class without fear I will continue to work with children.
I could have been your Madam President; Victoria Woodhull was counting on me

Joan didn't sleep with any man who had a draft card
A woman without a man is like a fish without a bicycle
I could have been your Madam President; Victoria Woodhull was counting on me
I would have kept abortion legal; honey, if men could get pregnant it would be a sacrament

A woman without a man is like a fish without a bicycle
I wasn't elected, but I can still sleep with the ex-President
I would have kept abortion legal; honey, if men could get pregnant
it would be a sacrament
I suppose I could have stayed home, baked cookies, hosted teas

For Hillary Rodham Clinton, Janet Reno, Mabel Dodge Luhan, Georgia O'Keeffe, Erica Jong, Joan Baez, Victoria Woodhull and Gloria Steinem.

Kate Marco

sparks

women,
words fly
from your mouths,
like sparks
from Liberty's torch,
lighting
the hearts
of sisters
around our mother earth,
burning
those who dare
stand close
to freedom's cause.

daughters,
come
bear witness
to your mothers' births,
shells crack
as spirits soar,
chains lie broken,
shining in the sun
of this new age.

sisters,
look into my face
and see your destiny,
we have nothing
save each other
and in that solitary truth,
we have it all.

Bios

Lisa Alvarado (34, 66) Award Winning Poet. Novelist. Journalist. Editor. Installation and Performance Artist. Foodie. Ethical Sensualist. Chicana. Jew. Published a novel with Penguin/NAL and 2 poetry volumes. Daughter of Oya. Hispanic Author of the Year 2009/State of Illinois.

Tani Arness (3) lives in Albuquerque, New Mexico finding beauty in the intersection of words and spirit. Her work appears in numerous literary magazines including *North American Review*, *Red Rock Review*, and *Crab Orchard Review*. A collection of her poems can be found in the poetry anthology, *Tzimtzum*. See www.tani-arness.com

H. Marie Aragón (100) was born on August 26th, Womens's Equality Day. On this day in 1920 the 19th. Amendment passed. Aragón lives and writes in Eldorado, New Mexico where she found gold in the writing community. Aragon's poetry has been published in numerous journals and anthologies. In 2014 her work was presented as a Mini Feature in the *Malpaís Review*. In 2015 she won the Lummox Poetry Prize, leading to a chapbook titled, *When Desert Willows Speak*.

Megan Baldrige (46) is a retired English teacher, gardener, Japanophile, museum-docenting, garden-loving mom of four grown children, who has lived in Connecticut half her life, and Cedar Crest and Albuquerque the better half of her life.

Joanne Bodin, PhD, (55) is an award-winning author and poet. Her book of poetry, *Piggybacked,* was a finalist in the New Mexico Book Awards. Her novel, *Walking Fish*, won the New Mexico Book Awards and the International Book Awards in gay/lesbian fiction. She is past vice president of the New Mexico State Poetry Society. Her poetry has appeared in numerous poetry anthologies.

Lindsay Brenner (24) is from St. Louis, Missouri originally. She came to Albuquerque in 2010 for a job and decided to stay. In 2014-2016 she served in the Peace Corps in Morocco. Her undergraduate degree is in studio art and she loves making things, writing, being outside, traveling and learning.

Nickole Brown's (92) first collection, *Sister*, was published by Red Hen Press, and *Fanny Says* came out from BOA Editions in 2015. Currently, she is the Editor for the Marie Alexander Series in Prose Poetry and is on faculty at the Great Smokies Writing Program at UNCA. She lives with her wife, poet Jessica Jacobs, in Asheville, NC.

Tina Carlson (5, 18, 40) is a poet and a psychiatric provider at Albuquerque Healthcare for the Homeless. Her book *Ground, Wind, This Body* (UNM Press, 2017) explores the vestiges of war that live in traumatized soldiers and their families.

Deborah Coy (93) has published three books and has been published in several anthologies and online poetry publications. She was an editor for the anthology, *La Llorona*, published by Beatlick Press, which won the New Mexico/Arizona Book Awards for Anthology in 2013.

Martha Deed (85) longs to spit fire but writes poems instead. Her newest chapbook is *We Should Have Seen This Coming (*locofo, 2017). Also, *Climate Change* (FootHills Publishing, 2014) *The Last Collaboration (*Furtherfield, 2012). Edited Millie Niss's poetry collection, *City Bird* (BlazeVox, 2010). Several chapbooks, anthologies, many poetry journals. http://sporkworld.tumblr.com/

Mary Dezember, Ph.D. (98), believes in freedom of expression, inclusivity, pluralism, and creating awareness that catalyzes healing. Professor of English, she teaches creative writing, art history and literature at New Mexico Institute of Mining and Technology. She is the author of two published books of poetry and of the website poetryaboutart.com.

Winner of the Southwest Writers poetry award and twice nominated for a Pushcart, **Katherine DiBella Seluja**'s (2) poetry has appeared in *bosque*, Crab Creek Review, Iron Horse Literary Review and Santa Ana River Review, among others. Her first collection, *Gather the Night*, focuses on mental illness and is forthcoming from UNM Press in 2018.

Upon completing an M.A. (English, SUNY, Stony Brook) **Mary Dudley** (10, 12) earned a Ph.D. (UNM, Psychological Foundations of Education), in early child development across cultures. She has written about and worked with young children, their families and teachers. Her poems have appeared in a number of collections.

Julie Dunleavy (53) is a poet living in Albuquerque, NM. She has published her poetry in a number of chap books, a photography/poetry book with Dick Ruddy, and in several anthologies. She has written award winning feature articles and professional writing in the mental health field.

Jesse Ehrenberg (80) transplanted to New Mexico from New York in the early 70's. He started writing poetry as a teenager and, as with any good obsession, has never found a reason to stop. He's been published in several New Mexico poetry anthologies, and has a book coming out this spring.

Judy Grahn (21) is best known as a poet, also as author of *Another Mother Tongue: Gay Words, Gay Worlds*, and a memoir *A Simple Revolution, the Making of an Activist Poet.* She teaches creative writing, mythology, and a new origin story based in ritual, when the spirit moves her. Next book, from Red Hen Press: *Hanging On Our Own Bones.*

Kenneth P. Gurney (83) lives in Albuquerque, NM, USA with his beloved Dianne. His latest collection of poems is *Stump Speech* (2015). He runs the poetry blog *Watermelon Isotope.* His personal website is at kpgurney.me.

Pamela Adams Hirst (36), aka Beatlick Pamela, moved to New Mexico from Nashville, Tennessee, and established award-winning Beatlick Press in order to posthumously publish her life partner's only book, *Backpack Trekker: A 60s Flashback*. As a book designer and publisher, seven volumes from her press have been named Finalists in the NM AZ Book Awards, with one first-place winner in Anthology 2013. Continuing the literary and performance legacy established by Beatlick Joe Speer, she currently writes and publishes from her home in Oaxaca, Mexico.

Ceinwen E. Cariad Haydon's (79) stories have been published on *Fiction on the Web, Literally Stories, StepAway* and *Alliterati.* Her poems are published in *Poems to Survive In, Writers Against Prejudice* and *I am not a Silent Poet.* She is studying for an MA in Creative Writing at Newcastle University.

Kathamann (96) is a returned Peace Corps Volunteer/Afghanistan and a retired registered nurse. She has been active in the Santa Fe arts community for 30 years, exhibiting in juried, group and solo exhibits (kathamann.com). Her poems have been published in local and national anthologies.

Herb Kauderer (56, 57) is an associate professor of English at Hilbert College and the author of eleven books of poetry. Like so many of us, he is the grandson of non-native English speaking immigrants. He is also the husband of a non-native English speaking immigrant. He has three daughters.

Mary Elizabeth Lang (58) is a retired college instructor. She earned her MFA from Bennington Writing Seminars. Her poems have appeared in many journals, including *Ekphrasis; The Prose Poem;* and *Comstock Review.* Her first book of poetry, *Under Red Cedars,* was published by Little Red Tree Publishing.

Gayle Lauradunn's (33, 48) debut poetry collection *Reaching for Air* was named a Finalist by the Texas Institute of Letters for Best First Book of Poetry. Her life has been devoted to social justice activism. She still hopes it has not been in vain.

Lyn Lifshin (1, 8) has published over 130 books and chapbooks including 3 from Black Press: *Cold Comfort, Before it's Light,* and *Another Woman who Looks Like Me.* Recent books include: *Secretariat: The Red Freak, The Miracle; Knife Edge & Absinthe: the Tango Poems. Malala; A Girl Goes into the Woods; Femme Eterna; Little Dancer: the Degas Poems* and *alivelikealoadedgun.* She edited 3 anthologies: *Tangled vines, Lips Unsealed; Ariadne's Thread.* Her web: www: lynlifshin.com

Jane Lipman's (52) first book, *On the Back Porch of the Moon*, Black Swan Editions, 2012, won the 2013 New Mexico/Arizona Book Award and a New Mexico Press Women's Award. Her chapbooks, *The Rapture of Tulips* and *White Crow's Secret Life*, were finalists for NM Book Awards in 2009 and 2010. She founded and directed Taos Institute, sponsoring workshops by Robert Bly, Joseph Campbell, Gioia Timpanelli, and others.

John Macker (9) is the author of eleven books of poetry, most recently, *Blood in the Mix* (w/El Paso poet Lawrence Welsh). He is contributing editor to Albuquerque's Malpais Review. Is currently contributing poems to Denver woodblock artist Leon Loughridge's folio series, *Gorge Songs,* about the Rio Grande gorge in Northern New Mexico.

Kate Marco (105) has been writing poetry, prose and short stories since she learned to put pen to paper. In 1976, Seven Stars published a small book of her poems, *Through The Changes, Gently* (published under the name Kathleen Keller), which reached #4 on the small press best-seller list. Kate has been published is many poetry journals, newspapers, magazines and periodicals for several decades. She was poetry editor for *Artlines* magazine in Taos, New Mexico.

Eliza Mimski (35, 94) lives and writes in San Francisco, California. Her work has appeared in *Fiction 365, Sparkle and Blink, Poets Reading the News, Entropy, New Verse News* as well as other publications. She has taken a renewed interest in writing poetry since the election. It helps to keep her sane.

Erin Lynn Marsh (22, 23) is a poet writing and teaching in Bemidji, MN. She earned her MFA in Creative Writing from Lesley University's low-residency MFA program in Boston, MA. She has published poems in Post Road Magazine, Sugar House Review, Paper Darts, CRE8, and Emrys Journal and others.

Poet, essayist, artist **Anne MacNaughton** (37, 89) writes, paints and teaches in New Mexico. Her work has been published in *The Notebook, The Best Poetry of 1989, Rag and Bone Shop of the Heart*, and *In Company: an Anthology of New Mexico Poets after 1960.* She co-founded S.O.M.O.S. and directed the Taos Poetry Circus.

Karla Linn Merrifield (97), a National Park Artist-in-Residence, has 12 books to her credit; the newest is *Bunchberries, More Poems of Canada.* She is assistant editor and book reviewer for *The Centrifugal Eye.* Give her name a Google to read more and visit her at http://karlalinn.blogspot.com.

Jude Moore (67) is a femme, queer person originally from Albuquerque, New Mexico, who now resides in Baltimore. They are a teacher at inner-city high schools in Washington, DC, and in their creative work, interested in exploring young queer identity and politics, with a lot of pop culture references. In their spare time, they enjoy listening to Banks, watching vines, and playing soccer with their partner and dog.

Merimee Moffitt (78, 102) writes to make sense of things, to investigate, to rant, to emote, to use a voice once silenced. Feminism is a no-brainer, she says, and losing the chance to have a woman for president is the biggest disappointment ever. She has published two books, *Making Little Edens* and *Free Love, Free Fall,* and is at work on a book about addiction called *Blame.*

Jules Nyquist (54, 103) is the founder of Jules' Poetry Playhouse, LLC, a place for poetry and play in Albuquerque, NM. She took her MFA in Writing and Literature from Bennington College, VT. She is an active member of her local NOW chapter and is waiting for the ERA amendment to pass soon. Her publications and interviews are listed on www.julesnyquist.com

Taos native **Kate Padilla's** (70) poetry and art reflects her extensive travel and New Mexican roots. She also blends her experience with political injustice and women's right. She now resides in Albuquerque.

Susan Paquet (76, 77) works as a lawyer, for fun she is a poet and short story writer. She currently lives in New Mexico, where she was raised. Susan's writing has been published in various journals and anthologies in New Mexico and Texas. She has also published the anthology, Apricots and Tortillas.

Stuart A. Paterson (82) is a widely published & anthologised Scottish poet living on the Galloway coast. His work has won various awards & his latest publication is *Aye* (Tapsalteerie Press 2016), his first Scots language collection. For nearly 30 years he's been writing about and actively supporting the campaign for Scottish independence. *Looking South,* poems about Galloway, will be published by Indigo Dreams in 2017. https://en-gb.facebook.com/patersonpoetry/

Colleen Powderly (42) began writing poetry in 1997. Early poems reflected her childhood in the deep South and years spent in the Midwest. Those poems eventually formed the basis for her book, *Split*, published by FootHills Publishing in 2009. More recent work has focused on stories from the working class, particularly from women's lives.

Sylvia Ramos Cruz (73) is a mother, grandmother, surgeon, women's rights activist, gardener, world traveler, friend and lover. Her poems, eclectic in form and content, are inspired by works of art in all its forms, women's lives, and every-day injustices. She loves words and what they can do.

Margaret Randall's (39) most recent book of poems is She Becomes Time (Wings Press, 2016). A new collection, The Morning After: Poetry and Prose in a Post-Truth World, will be out from Wings Press in September 2017. She has been translating, including Only the Road / Solo el Camino: Eight Decades of Cuban Poetry (Duke University Press, 2016), and individual collections by Cuban poets: Alfredo Zaldívar and Laura Ruiz Montes (Red Mountain Press, Santa Fe, New Mexico, 2017) and Chely Lima (The Operating System, Brooklyn, NY, 2017). Duke also just released her most recent title, an essay on Cuban internationalism: Exporting Revolution: Cuba's Global Solidarity.

Stella Reed (65) is from Santa Fe, NM. She is a teacher for WingSpan Poetry Project bringing weekly poetry classes to domestic violence and homeless shelters. Latest and forthcoming poems appear in *Slipstream* and the *Bellingham Review.*

John Roche (75, 88) is the author of *On Conesus, Topicalities, Road Ghosts, and The Joe Poems: The Continuing Saga of Joe the Poet*, as well as the author of *Mo' Joe: The Anthology*. He believes we are going to need poetry to get through the next four years or forty years.

Janet Ruth (30) is an emeritus research ornithologist from Corrales, NM. She has published scientific papers on bird ecology and natural history essays in bird magazines. Her writing focuses on connections to the natural world. She has poems recently published in *Grey Sparrow Journal* and in the anthology *VALUE: Essays, Stories & Poems by Women of A Certain Age* (Beatlick Press).

Georgia Santa Maria (69) is a Native New Mexican, and has been an artist and writer most of her life. In 2012 she was a Guest Editor for LUMMOX Poetry Anthology, Issue I. She has two books, *Lichen Kisses* (2013), and *Dowsing*, just out. Recently, she was first runner-up for the LUMMOX 5 Poetry Prize.

Elaine G. Schwartz (62) resides in Albuquerque, NM with her husband, Daniel Schwartz, and Purr'l, the Postmodern Pussy Cat. Her writing, described as a tapestry of place and political imagination, has appeared in numerous publications including the *Santa Fe Literary Review, Malpais Review* and *Persimmon Tree.*

Lauren Schwartz (38, 91) is a New York City-based poet and photographer. Her social work with low-income senior citizens in The Bronx is the subject of her latest project, Aging in Place; a collection photographs and poetry.

Patricia Roth Schwartz (6, 26) is a poet and writer of fiction and creative non-fiction from New York's Finger Lakes. Widely published in small press journals, she also has seven books of poems. Her latest are *Charleston Girls, a Memoir in Poems of a West Virginia Childhood,* and *The Crows of Copper John, a History of Auburn Prison in Poems,* plus a chapbook, *Know Better: poems of resistance.*

Celeste Helene Schantz (15) has work which appears in Stone Canoe, One Throne Magazine, Mud Season Review and others. She has studied with Marge Piercy and Kim Addonizio. She lives in Upstate New York with her son Evan and is currently working on her first book of poetry.

Gretchen Schulz (72) is an Activist Artist at Large.

Eddie Swayze (44) is a poet, performing artist, actor, and visual artist. He performs with the ASL poetry troupe Dangerous Signs and has also acted in many theatrical productions. He graduated with a Master of Fine Arts degree from the Rochester Institute of Technology in 1995. His forthcoming poetry book is called *Futuropolis.*

Roslye Ultan (29) draws on her visual background, and interest in nature to write poetry on the wonders of everyday life. She fills a white page with color, form, and the rhythm of existence.

Denise Weaver Ross (xii, 17, 19) is an artist, poet and graphic designer who lives and works in Albuquerque, NM. Denise graduated from UMass-Amherst with an MFA, regularly exhibits in the Southwest, and contributes her design abilities to local writers, artists and galleries. Her art and poetry can be found in many local and international magazines and anthologies.

Liza Wolff-Francis (50) was co-director for the 2014 Austin International Poetry Festival and a member of the 2008 Albuquerque Poetry Slam Team. Her work most recently appeared in Bearing the Mask, Rock the Chair, and Poetry Pacific. She has a chapbook out called Language of Crossing (2015, Swimming with Elephants Publications).

Scott Wiggerman, (59) an editor for Dos Gatos Press, is the author of three books of poetry, *Leaf and Beak: Sonnets, Presence,* and *Vegetables and Other Relationships*; and the editor of several volumes, including *Wingbeats: Exercises & Practice in Poetry, Lifting the Sky: Southwestern Haiku & Haiga,* and *Bearing the Mask.*

Dwain Wilder's (14) publications include *Under the Only Moon*, poems in *Kudzu Review, Shadow/Play, Le Mot Juste, Lake Affect, Hot Air* and *Zen Bow.* He is past editor of *Zen Bow*, and co-edited *Liberty's Vigil: The Occupy Anthology*, and *Vigil for the Marcellus Shale.* Dwain lives in a small cottage beside a large dark forest.

Holly Wilson (32) lives in Albuquerque, New Mexico, where she has been active in the poetry community for many years. She is one of the members of the Beatlick Sisters, a multimedia performance poetry duo. Politics is one of her favorite topics to talk and write about.

Leah Zazulyer (63) writes poetry, prose, translates Yiddish poetry, and was a special education teacher and school psychologist. She lives in Rochester, New York, but grew up in California in a bilingual family from Belarus. Publications include five poetry books, and two books of translations of Israel Emiot. This project is terrific!

Professor **Kevin Zepper** (20) teaches at Minnesota State University Moorhead. He has authored four chapbooks of poetry and is a part of the music/poetry duo Lines&Notes. Some of his recent photo credits include: Red Weather, Inscape and Portage Magazine.

BEATLICK PRESS

Writers with Something to Say
Beatlick Press was established in 2011 to honor the memory of Beatlick Joe Speer of Albuquerque, New Mexico and continue his artistic mission to publish deserving writers:

Pamela Adams Hirst, publisher
Beatlick Press
Albuquerque, NM
http://beatlick.com/

&

JULES POETRY PLAYHOUSE PUBLICATIONS
Jules Nyquist is the founder and operator of Jules' Poetry Playhouse in Albuquerque, NM, a place for poetry and play
http://www.julesnyquist.com

43862438R00080

Made in the USA
Middletown, DE
21 May 2017